REALLY EASY GUITAR

THE BEATLES FOR KIDS

14 SONGS WITH CHORDS, LYRICS & BASIC TAB

Cover photo © Michael Ochs Archives / Getty Images

ISBN 978-1-5400-9337-0

Visit Hal Leonard Online at
www.halleonard.com

Contact us:
Hal Leonard
7777 West Bluemound Road
Milwaukee, WI 53213
Email: info@halleonard.com

In Europe, contact:
Hal Leonard Europe Limited
42 Wigmore Street
Marylebone, London, W1U 2RN
Email: info@halleonardeurope.com

In Australia, contact:
Hal Leonard Australia Pty. Ltd.
4 Lentara Court
Cheltenham, Victoria, 3192 Australia
Email: info@halleonard.com.au

All My Loving

Words and Music by John Lennon and Paul McCartney

(Capo 2nd Fret)

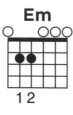
Em

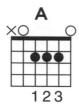
A

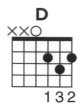
D

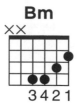
Bm

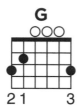
G

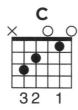
C

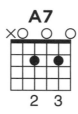
A7

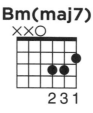
Bm(maj7)

VERSE 1

Moderately fast

```
          Em        A        D          Bm
Close your eyes    and I'll kiss   you, tomorrow I'll miss      you.

    G           Em      C     A7
Remember I'll always be true.

          Em        A        D          Bm
And then while I'm away,    I'll write home every day,

        G          A           D
and I'll send all my loving to you.
```

VERSE 2

```
          Em          A       D           Bm
I'll pretend     that I'm kiss - ing the lips I am miss - ing,

    G           Em          C     A7
and hope that my dreams will come true.

          Em      A       D           Bm
And then while I'm away, I'll write home every day,

        G          A           D
and I'll send all my loving to you.
```

BRIDGE

```
    Bm     Bm(maj7)              D
All my lovin', I          will send to you.

    Bm     Bm(maj7)       D
All my lovin', dar - lin', I'll be true.
```

GUITAR SOLO

| G | | | D | | | |
| A7 | | | D | | N.C. | |

VERSE 3

           Em   **A**   **D**   **Bm**
Close your eyes   and I'll kiss   you, tomorrow I'll miss   you.

     G   **Em**   **C**   **A7**
Remember I'll always be true.

          Em   **A**   **D**   **Bm**
And then while I'm away,   I'll write home every day,

     G   **A**   **D**
and I'll send all my loving to you.

REPEAT BRIDGE

OUTRO

    Bm   **D**
All my lovin', all my   lovin',

    Bm   **D**
oo, all my lovin', I will send to   you.

All You Need Is Love

Words and Music by John Lennon and Paul McCartney

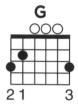
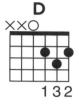
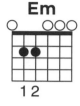

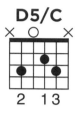
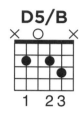
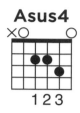
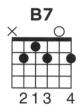
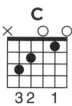

G   **D**   **Em**   **D7**   **Am**

D5/C   **D5/B**   **Asus4**   **B7**   **C**

INTRO

Moderately

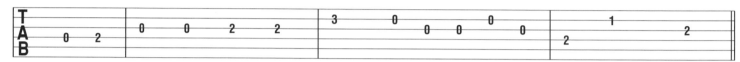

INTERLUDE 1

G	D	Em
Love,	love,	love.

G	D	Em
Love,	love,	love.

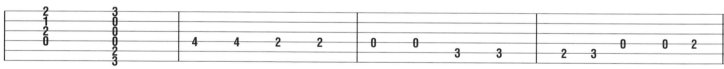

Love,   love,   love.

VERSE 1

G   **D**   **Em**
There's nothing you can do that can't be done.

G   **D**   **Em**
Nothing you can sing that can't be sung.

D7   **G**   **D**   **Am**
Nothing you can say, but you can learn how to play the game.

     D   **D5/C**   **D5/B**   **D**
It's easy.

VERSE 2

```
G                   D              Em
  Nothing you can make that can't be made.

G        D              Em
  No one you can save that can't be saved.

D7               G                D                    Am
  Nothing you can do, but you can learn how to be you in time.

    D     D5/C   D5/B   D
It's easy.
```

CHORUS

```
G        Asus4        D
  All you need is love.

G        Asus4        D
  All you need is love.

G        B7          Em
  All you need is love,    love.

C        D         G
  Love is all you need.
```

REPEAT INTERLUDE

REPEAT CHORUS

VERSE 3

```
G                       D              Em
  There's nothing you can know that isn't known.

G        D              Em
  Nothing you can see that isn't shown.

D7                       G          D              Am
  There's nowhere you can be  that isn't where you're meanto be.

    D     D5/C   D5/B   D
It's easy.
```

REPEAT CHORUS (2 TIMES)

OUTRO

```
        G
Love is all you need. Love is all you need.


Love is all you need. Love is all you need.
```

Eight Days a Week

Words and Music by John Lennon and Paul McCartney

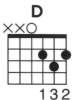 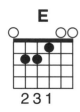 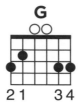  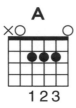

D   E   G   Bm   A

INTRO

Moderately

| D | E | G | D |

VERSE 1

D   E   G   D
Oo, I need your love, babe. Guess you know it's true.

               E   G   D
Hope you need my love, babe, just like I need you.

Bm   G   Bm   E
Hold me, love me. Hold me, love me.

D   E   G   D
I ain't got nothing but love, babe,   eight days a week.

VERSE 2

D   E   G   D
Love you ev'ry day,   girl, always on my mind.

             E   G   D
One thing I can say,   girl, love you all the time.

Bm   G   Bm   E
Hold me, love me. Hold me, love me.

D   E   G   D
I ain't got nothing but love, girl,   eight days a week.

BRIDGE

A   Bm
Eight days a week, I love   you.

E   G   A
Eight days a week is not enough to show I care.

VERSE 3

```
D           E      G              D
Oo, I need your love, babe. Guess you know it's true.

                    E      G              D
Hope you need my love, babe, just like I need you,   oh.

Bm    G      Bm      E
Hold me, love me. Hold me, love me.

  D              E      G              D
I ain't got nothing but love, babe,   eight days a week.
```

BRIDGE

```
A                    Bm
Eight days a week, I love   you

E              G        A
Eight days a week is not enough to show I care.
```

VERSE 4

```
D              E    G              D
Love you ev'ry day,   girl, always on my mind.

                    E    G              D
One thing I can say,   girl, love you all the time.

Bm    G      Bm      E
Hold me, love me. Hold me, love me.

  D              E      G              D
I ain't got nothing but love, girl,   eight days a week.
```

OUTRO

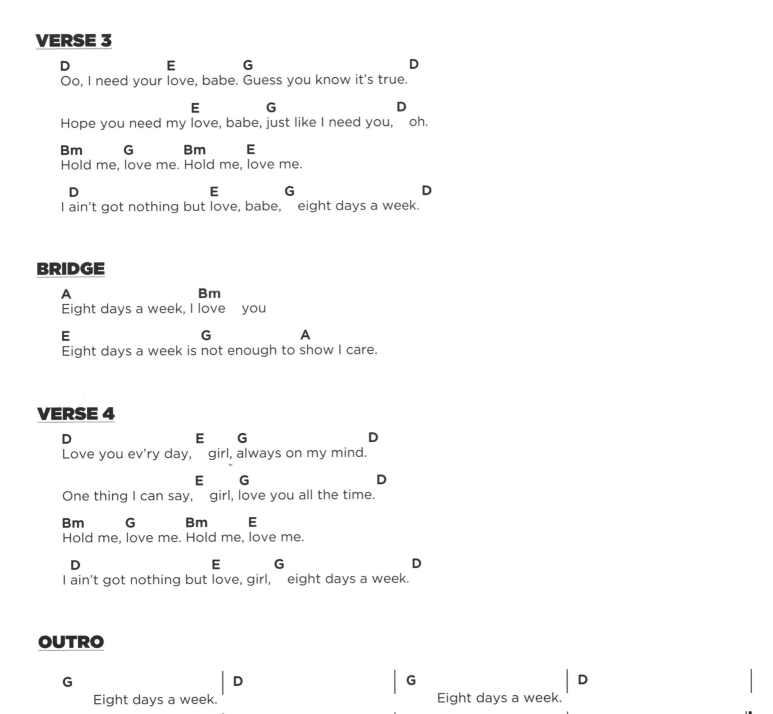

```
G                    | D            | G            | D            |          |
   Eight days a week.                   Eight days a week.

D                    | E            | G            | D            |          ‖
```

Good Day Sunshine

Words and Music by John Lennon and Paul McCartney

(Capo 2nd Fret)

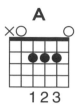
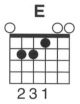
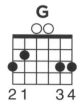

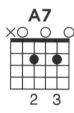
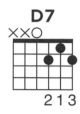
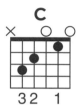
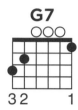
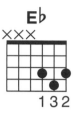

INTRO

Moderately

D | | | ||

CHORUS

A   E
Good day sunshine.

A   E
Good day sunshine.

D
Good day sunshine.

VERSE 1

N.C.   G   E7   A7
I need to laugh   and when the sun is out

D7   G
I've got something I can   laugh about.

            E7   A7
I feel good   in a special way.

D7   G
I'm in love and it's a   sunny day.

<u>REPEAT CHORUS</u>

VERSE 2

```
N.C.        G    E7         A7
We take a walk     the sun is shining down,

D7                              G
burns my feet as they touch    the ground.
```

INTERLUDE

```
C           A7      | D7              | G7              | C              ‖
```

REPEAT CHORUS

VERSE 3

```
N.C.        G    E7         A7
Then we lie       beneath a shady tree.

D7                         G
I love her and she's loving me.

                     E7              A7
She feels good.        She knows she's looking fine.

D7                         G
I'm so proud to know that    she is mine.
```

REPEAT CHORUS (2 times)

OUTRO

```
Eb
Good day sun - shine.     Good    day sun - shine.
                 (Good      day sun - shine.     Good    day sun - shine.)
```

Hey Jude

Words and Music by John Lennon and Paul McCartney

(Capo 3rd Fret)

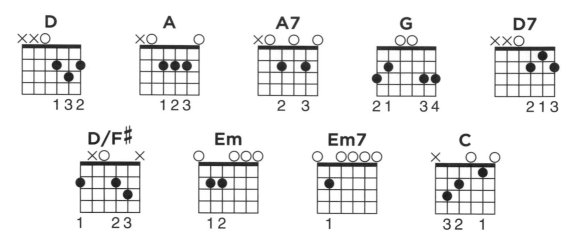

VERSE 1

Moderately

D · · · · · · · · · · A · · · · · A7 · · · · · · · · · · · D
Hey Jude, don't make it bad. Take a sad song and make it better.

G · · · · · · · · · · · · · · · · · D · · · · · · · · · · · · · A7 · · · · · · · D
Remember to let her into your heart, then you can start   to make it better.

VERSE 2

D · · · · · · · · · · A · · · · · A7 · · · · · · · · · · · D
Hey Jude, don't be afraid. You were made to go out and get her.

G · D · · · · · · · · A7 · · · · · · · D
The minute you let her under your skin, then you begin   to make it better.

D7
And any time you feel the pain,

BRIDGE 1

G · · · · · · D/F♯ · · · · Em · · · · · Em7 · · · · · A7 · · · · · · · · · D
hey Jude,   refrain.   Don't carry the world   upon your shoulders.

D7
For well you know that it's a fool

G · · · · · · D/F♯ · · · · Em · · · · · Em7 · · · · · A7 · · · · · · · · D
who plays   it cool   by making his world   a little colder.

D7 · · · · A7
Na, na, na, na, na, na, na, na, na.

VERSE 3

D   A   A7   D
Hey Jude, don't let me down.   You have   found her now go and get her.

G   D   A7   D
Remember to let her into your heart, then you can start   to make it better.

D7
So let it out and let it in,

BRIDGE 2

G   D/F♯   Em   Em7   A7   D
hey Jude,   begin.   You're waiting for someone to perform   with.

D7
And don't you know that it's just you,

G   D/F♯   Em   Em7   A7   D
hey Jude,   you'll do.   The movement you need   is on your shoulder.

D7   A7
Na, na, na, na, na, na, na, na, na, yeah.

VERSE 4

D   A   A7   D
Hey Jude,   don't make it bad. Take a sad song and make it better.

G   D   A7   D
Remember to let her under your skin, then you begin   to make it better,

better, better, better, better, better, oh.

OUTRO

Repeat and fade

‖: D | C | G | D   :‖
Na,   na,   na,   na, na, na, na.   Na, na, na, na. Hey Jude.

I Want to Hold Your Hand

Words and Music by John Lennon and Paul McCartney

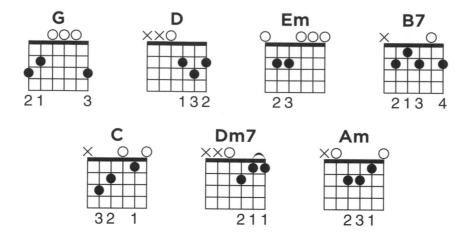

INTRO

Moderately

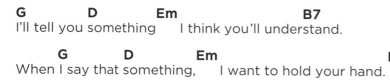

Oh   yeah,

VERSE 1

G   **D**   **Em**   **B7**
I'll tell you something   I think you'll understand.

G   **D**   **Em**   **B7**
When I say that something,   I want to hold your hand.

C   **D**   **G**   **Em**   **C**   **D**   **G**
I want to hold your hand.   I want to hold your hand.

VERSE 2

G   **D**   **Em**   **B7**
Oh, please say to me   you'll let me be your man.

G   **D**   **Em**   **B7**
And please say to me,   you'll let me hold your hand.

C   **D**   **G**   **Em**   **C**   **D**   **G**
Now let me hold your hand.   I want to hold your hand.

BRIDGE 1

Dm7   **G**   **C**   **Am**
And when I touch you I feel happy inside.

Dm7   **G**   **C**   **D**   **C**   **D**   **C**   **D**
It's such a feeling that my love, I can't hide,   I can't hide,   I can't hide.

VERSE 3

G   D   Em   B7
Yeah, you got that something I think you'll understand.

G   D   Em   B7
When I say that something, I want to hold your hand.

C   D   G Em C   D   G
I want to hold your hand.   I want to hold your hand.

BRIDGE 2

Dm7   G   C   Am
  And when I touch you I feel happy inside.

Dm7   G   C   D C   D   C   D
  It's such a feeling that my love, I can't hide, I can't hide, I can't hide.

VERSE 4

G   D   Em   B7
Yeah, you got that something I think you'll understand.

G   D   Em   B7
When I say that something, I want to hold your hand.

C   D   G Em C   D   B7
I want to hold your hand.   I want to hold your hand.

C   D   C   G
I want to hold your hand.

In My Life

Words and Music by John Lennon and Paul McCartney

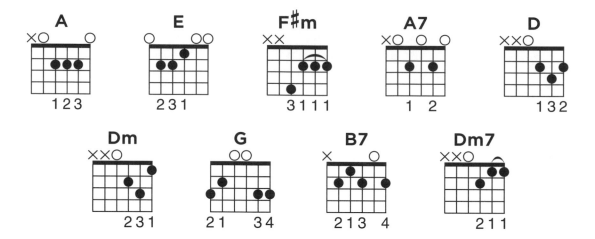

INTRO

Moderately

There are

VERSE 1

A   E F#m   A7   D Dm   A

places I remember   all my life,   though some have changed.

            E   F#m A7   D   Dm   A

Some forever, not for better.   Some have gone   and some remain.

CHORUS 1

      F#m   D   G   A

All these places had their moments with lovers and friends. I still can recall.

      F#m   B7   Dm7   A

Some are dead and some are living. In my life, I've loved them all.

INTERLUDE 1

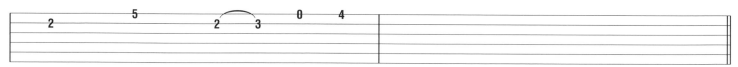

But of

VERSE 2

A   E   F#m A7   D Dm   A
all these friends and lovers   there is no one compares with you.

                  E   F#m   A7   D   Dm   A
And these memories lose their meaning   when I think of love as something new.

CHORUS 2

         F#m   D   G   A
Though I know I'll never lose affection for people and things that went before.

F#m   B7   Dm7 A
I know I'll often stop and think about them. In my life I love you more.

INTERLUDE 2

A   E | F#m   A7 | D   Dm | A |

        E | F#m   A7 | D   Dm | A   ‖

Though I

CHORUS 3

F#m   D   G   A
know I'll never lose affection for people and things that went before.

F#m   B7   Dm7 A
I know I'll often stop and think about them. In my life I love you more.

OUTRO

In

Dm7
my life I love you

more.

Let It Be

Words and Music by John Lennon and Paul McCartney

C 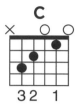 G 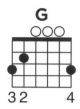 Am  F 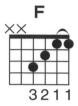 C/G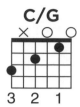

3 2 1   3 2   4   2 3 1   3 2 1 1   3 2 1

INTRO

Moderately

C   G | Am   F | C   G | F   C ||

When I

VERSE 1

C   G   Am   F
find myself in times   of trouble, Mother Mary comes   to me,

C   G   F   C
speaking words of wisdom, let it be.

                G   Am   F
And in my hour of darkness she is standing right in front   of me,

C   G   F   C
speaking words of wisdom, let it be.

CHORUS 1

            Am   C/G   F   C
Let it be,   let it be,   let it be,   let it be.

                        G   F   C
    Whisper words of wisdom, let it be.

VERSE 2

        C   G   Am   F
And when the broken hearted people living in the world   agree,

C   G   F   C
there will be an answer, let it be.

                            G   Am   F
For though they may be parted,   there is still a chance that they   will see,

C   G   F   C
there will be an answer, let it be.

CHORUS 2

             Am   C/G   F   C
Let it be,   let it be,   let it be,   let it be.

                        G   F   C
Yeah, there will be an answer, let it be.

             Am   C/G   F   C
Let it be,   let it be,   let it be,   let it be.

                        G   F   C
1. Whis - per words of wisdom, let it be.
2. There will   be   an answer, let it be.

INTERLUDE

GUITAR SOLO

    C   G | Am   F | C   G | F   C |

           G | Am   F | C   G | F   C

REPEAT CHORUS 1

VERSE 3

        C   G   Am   F
And when the night is cloudy, there is still a light that shines   on me,

C   G   F   C
shine until tomorrow, let it be.

                         G   Am   F
I wake up to the sound   of music, Mother Mary comes   to me,

C   G   F   C
speaking words of wisdom, let it be.

REPEAT CHORUS 2

REPEAT CHORUS 1

OUTRO

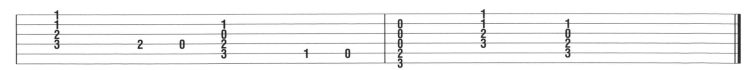

Love Me Do

Words and Music by John Lennon and Paul McCartney

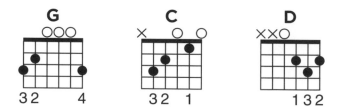

INTRO

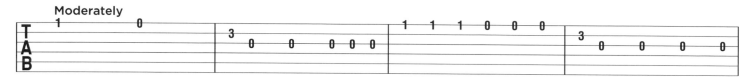

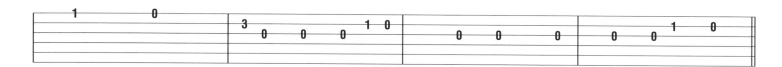

VERSE 1

G   C
Love, love me do.

     G   C
You know I love you.

     G   C
I'll always be true.   So, please,

N.C.   G   C   G   C
     love me do.   Oh, love me do.

VERSE 2

G   C
Love, love me do.

     G   C
You know I love you.

     G   C
I'll always be true.   So, please,

N.C.   G   C   G
     love me do.   Oh, love me do.

BRIDGE

D   C   G
Someone to love, somebody new.

D   C   G   N.C.
Someone to love, someone like you.

VERSE 3

G   C
Love, love me do.

      G   C
You know I love you.

      G   C
I'll always be true.   So, please,

N.C.   G   C   G
    love me do.   Oh, love   me do.

INTERLUDE

‖: D | | C | G |

| | | | N.C. D   ‖

VERSE 4

G   C
Love, love me do.

      G   C
You know I love you.

      G   C
I'll always be true.   So, please,

N.C.   G   C   G   C
    love me do.   Oh, love   me do.

      G   C   G   C
Yeah, love me do.   Oh love me do.

      G   *Fade*
Yeah, love me do.

Octopus's Garden

Words and Music by Richard Starkey

(Capo 4th Fret)

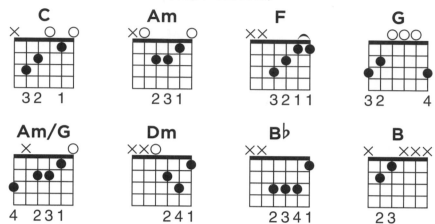

INTRO

Moderately, in 2

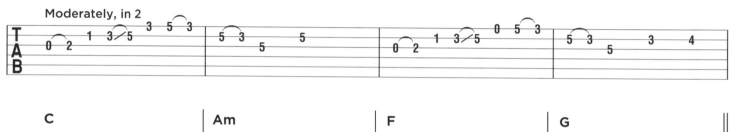

| C | | Am | | F | | G | |

VERSE 1

C   Am   F   G
I'd like to be   under the sea in an octopus's garden in the shade.

C   Am   F   G
He'd let us in,   knows where we've been, in his octopus's garden in the shade.

PRE-CHORUS 1

Am   Am/G F   G
I'd ask my friends to come and see   an octopus's garden with me.

CHORUS 1

C   Am   F   G   C
I'd like to be   under the sea in an octopus's garden in the shade.

VERSE 2

C   Am   F   G
We would be warm   below the storm in our little hide away beneath the waves.

C   Am   F   G
Resting our head   on the sea bed in an octopus's garden near a cave.

PRE-CHORUS 2

Am   Am/G F   G
    We would sing and dance around   because we know we can't be found.

CHORUS 2

C   Am   F   G   C
   I'd like to be   under the sea in an octopus's garden in the shade.

INTERLUDE

F | |Dm | |Bb | |C | |
Ah,   ah,   ah,   Ah,   ah, ah.

F | |Dm | |Bb |C |F |G ||
Ah,   ah,   ah,   Ah,   ah.

VERSE 3

C   Am   F   G
   We would shout   and swim about the coral that lies beneath the waves.

C   Am   F   G
   Oh, what joy for every girl and boy knowing they're happy and they're safe.

PRE-CHORUS 3

Am   Am/G F   G
    We would be so happy, you and me,   no one there to tell us what to do.

CHORUS 3

C   Am   F   G
   I'd like to be   under the sea in an octopus's garden with

Am Am/G   F   G
you,   in an octopus's garden with

Am Am/G   F   G   C N.C. B C
you,   in an octopus's garden with you.

With a Little Help from My Friends

Words and Music by John Lennon and Paul McCartney

(Capo 2nd Fret)

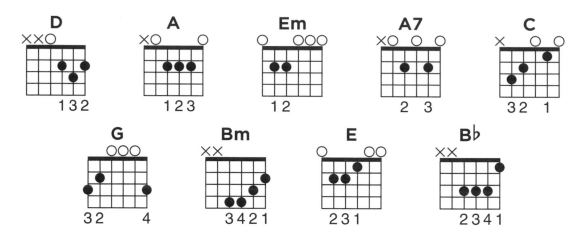

INTRO

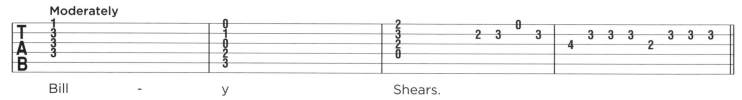

Bill - y   Shears.

VERSE 1

D   A   Em   A7   D
What would you think   if I sang   out of tune, would you stand up and walk   out on me?

A   Em   A7   D
Lend me your ears   and I'll sing   you a song and I'll try not to sing   out of key.

CHORUS 1

C   G   D
Oh, I get by   with a little help   from my friends.

C   G   D
Mmm, I get high   with a little help   from my friends.

G   D   A
Mmm, gonna try   with a little help from my friends.

VERSE 2

D   A   Em   A7   D
What do I do   when my love   is away? Does it worry you to be alone?

A   Em   A7   D
How do I feel   by the end   of the day? Are you sad because you're on your own?

CHORUS 2

```
             C              G            D
No, I get by    with a little help    from my friends.

              C              G            D
Mmm, get high    with a little help    from my friends.

               G                          D
Mmm, gonna try    with a little help from my friends.
```

BRIDGE 1

```
          Bm     E      D        C          G
Do you need    anybody?   I need somebody to love.

          Bm     E     D        C         G
Could it be    anybody?   I want somebody to love.
```

VERSE 3

```
D                 A       Em                                      A7        D
Would you believe    in a love     at first sight? Yes, I'm certain that it happens all the time.

                  A            Em                             A7         D
What do you see     when you turn     out the lights? I can't tell you but I know    it's mine.
```

CHORUS 3

```
             C              G            D
Oh, I get by    with a little help    from my friends.

              C              G            D
Mmm, get high    with a little help    from my friends.

               G                          D
Oh, I'm gonna try    with a little help from my friends.
```

BRIDGE 2

```
          Bm     E     D       C          G
Do you need    anybody?   I just need someone to love.

          Bm     E     D        C        G
Could it be    anybody?   I want somebody to love.
```

CHORUS 4

```
             C              G            D
Oh, I get by    with a little help    from my friends.

               C             G             D
Mmm, gonna try    with a little help    from my friends.

               G                          D
Oh, I get high,    with a little help from my friends.

             C                 G                    B♭  C   D
Yes, I get by    with a little help from my friends,    with a little help from my friends.
```

Yellow Submarine

Words and Music by John Lennon and Paul McCartney

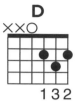 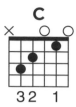 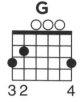   

D   **C**   **G**   **Em**   **Am**   **D7**

1 3 2   3 2   1   3 2   4   2 3   2 3 1   2 1 3

VERSE 1

Moderately

        D   C G Em Am   C   D7
In the town where I was born lived a man who sailed to sea.

G   D   C   G Em Am   C   D7
And he told   us of his life   in the land of submarines.

G   D   C   G Em Am   C   D7
So we sailed on to the sun 'til we found the sea of green.

G   D   C   G   Em Am   C   D7
And we lived beneath the waves in our yellow submarine.

CHORUS 1

G   D   G
We all live in a yellow submarine, yellow submarine, yellow submarine.

                      D   G
We all live in a yellow submarine, yellow submarine, yellow submarine.

VERSE 2

         D   C G   Em Am   C   D7
And our friends are all aboard, many more of them live next door.

G   D   C   G   Em Am   C D7
And the band begins to   play.

REPEAT CHORUS 1

INTERLUDE

```
D            C   | G         Em  | Am      C    | D7      G       |
D            C   | G         Em  | Am      C    | D7
```

VERSE 3

```
G    D     C   G   Em   Am                    C    D7
As we live a life of ease, every one of us      has   all we need.
              Spoken: (Every one of    us          has all we need.
G    D              C   G         Em   Am      C    D7
Sky of blue         and sea of green,     in our yellow      submarine.
     Sky of blue            sea of green,       in our yellow        submarine, ah hah!)
```

REPEAT CHORUS 1 AND FADE

Yesterday

Words and Music by John Lennon and Paul McCartney

(Capo 5th Fret)

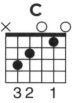 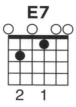 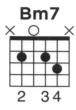 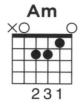 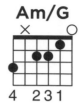 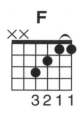

C   Bm7   E7   Am   Am/G   F

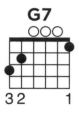 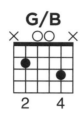 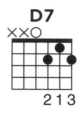 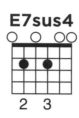 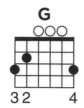 

G7   G/B   D7   E7sus4   G   Dm6

INTRO

Moderately

| C | | | | |

VERSE 1

C   **Bm7**   **E7**   **Am**   **Am/G**
Yesterday,   all my troubles seemed so far away.

F   **G7**   **F**   **C**   **G/B**
 Now it looks   as though they're here to stay.

    Am   **D7**   **F**   **C**
Oh, I believe   in yesterday.

VERSE 2

C   **Bm7**   **E7**   **Am**   **Am/G**
Suddenly,   I'm not half the man I used to be.

F   **G7**   **F**   **C**   **G/B**
 There's a shadow hanging o - ver me.

    Am   **D7**   **F**   **C**
Oh, yesterday   came suddenly.

BRIDGE 1

E7sus4   **E7**   **Am**   **G**   **F**   **Am**   **Dm6**   **G7**   **C**
Why   she   had   to   go,   I don't know, she wouldn't say.

E7sus4   **E7**   **Am**   **G**   **F**   **Am**   **Dm6**   **G7**   **C**
I   said   something wrong, now I long   for   yesterday.

VERSE 3

C   Bm7   E7   Am   Am/G
Yesterday,   love was such an easy game to play.

F   G7   F   C   G/B
 Now I need   a place to hide away. Oh,

Am   D7 F C
I believe   in yesterday.

BRIDGE 2

E7sus4 E7 Am G   F   Am   Dm6   G7   C
Why   she had to   go,   I don't know, she wouldn't say.

E7sus4 E7 Am G   F   Am   Dm6   G7 C
I   said something wrong, now I long for yesterday.

VERSE 4

C   Bm7   E7   Am   Am/G
Yesterday,   love was such an easy game to play.

F   G7   F   C   G/B
 Now I need   a place to hide away.

   Am   D7 F C
Oh, I believe   in yesterday.

     D7   F C
Mmm.

You've Got to Hide Your Love Away

Words and Music by John Lennon and Paul McCartney

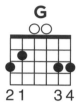
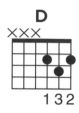
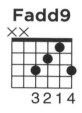
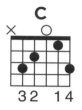
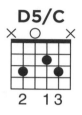

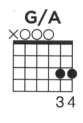
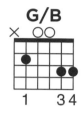
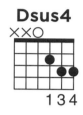

INTRO

Moderately, in 2

G   ‖

VERSE 1

G   D   Fadd9 G   C   Fadd9   C
Here I stand, head in hand, turn my face to the wall.

G   D   Fadd9 G   C   Fadd9   C   D
If she's gone, I can't go on, feeling two foot small.

VERSE 2

G   D   Fadd9 G   C   Fadd9   C
Everywhere people stare each and every day.

G   D   Fadd9 G   C   Fadd9   C   D   D5/C D5/B D5/A
I can see them laugh at me, and I hear them say,

CHORUS 1

G   G/A G/B C   Dsus4   D   Dsus2   D
"Hey! You've got   to   hide your love away.

G   G/A G/B C   Dsus4   D   Dsus2   D
Hey! You've got   to   hide your love away."

VERSE 3

```
G          D  Fadd9 G  C               Fadd9      C
How can I   even    try? I can never win.

G          D  Fadd9 G  C               Fadd9   C  D
Hearing them, seeing  them, in the state I'm in.
```

VERSE 4

```
G          D  Fadd9 G  C               Fadd9      C
How could she say to   me, "Love will find a way?"

G          D  Fadd9 G    C             Fadd9   C  D  D5/C  D5/B  D5/A
Gather 'round all you  clowns, let me hear you say,
```

CHORUS 2

```
G            G/A G/B C           Dsus4   D  Dsus2   D
"Hey! You've got   to     hide your love away.

G            G/A G/B C           Dsus4   D  Dsus2   D
Hey! You've got   to     hide your love away."
```

OUTRO

```
‖: G      D    | Fadd9   G    | C              | Fadd9   C    :‖ G            ‖
```

GUITAR NOTATION LEGEND

Chord Diagrams

CHORD DIAGRAMS graphically represent the guitar fretboard to show correct chord fingerings.

- The letter above the diagram tells the name of the chord.
- The top, bold horizontal line represents the nut of the guitar. Each thin horizontal line represents a fret. Each vertical line represents a string; the low E string is on the far left and the high E string is on the far right.
- A dot shows where to put your fret-hand finger and the number at the bottom of the diagram tells which finger to use.
- The "O" above the string means play it open, while an "X" means don't play the string.

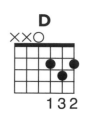

Tablature

TABLATURE graphically represents the guitar fingerboard. Each horizontal line represents a string, and each number represents a fret.

4th string, 2nd fret 1st & 2nd strings open, played together open D chord

Definitions for Special Guitar Notation

HAMMER-ON: Strike the first (lower) note with one finger, then sound the higher note (on the same string) with another finger by fretting it without picking.

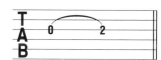

PULL-OFF: Place both fingers on the notes to be sounded. Strike the first note and without picking, pull the finger off to sound the second (lower) note.

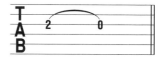

LEGATO SLIDE: Strike the first note and then slide the same fret-hand finger up or down to the second note. The second note is not struck.

SHIFT SLIDE: Same as legato slide, except the second note is struck.

Additional Musical Definitions

N.C.   • No chord. Instrument is silent.

   • Repeat measures between signs.

EASY GUITAR
WITH NOTES & TAB

This series features simplified arrangements with notes, tab, chord charts, and strum and pick patterns.

MIXED FOLIOS

00702287	Acoustic	$19.99
00702002	Acoustic Rock Hits for Easy Guitar	$17.99
00702166	All-Time Best Guitar Collection	$29.99
00702232	Best Acoustic Songs for Easy Guitar	$16.99
00119835	Best Children's Songs	$16.99
00703055	The Big Book of Nursery Rhymes & Children's Songs	$16.99
00698978	Big Christmas Collection	$19.99
00702394	Bluegrass Songs for Easy Guitar	$15.99
00289632	Bohemian Rhapsody	$19.99
00703387	Celtic Classics	$16.99
00224808	Chart Hits of 2016-2017	$14.99
00267383	Chart Hits of 2017-2018	$14.99
00334293	Chart Hits of 2019-2020	$16.99
00403479	Chart Hits of 2021-2022	$16.99
00702149	Children's Christian Songbook	$9.99
00702028	Christmas Classics	$9.99
00101779	Christmas Guitar	$16.99
00702141	Classic Rock	$8.95
00159642	Classical Melodies	$12.99
00253933	Disney/Pixar's Coco	$19.99
00702203	CMT's 100 Greatest Country Songs	$34.99
00702283	The Contemporary Christian Collection	$16.99

00196954	Contemporary Disney	$19.99
00702239	Country Classics for Easy Guitar	$24.99
00702257	Easy Acoustic Guitar Songs	$17.99
00702041	Favorite Hymns for Easy Guitar	$12.99
00222701	Folk Pop Songs	$19.99
00126894	Frozen	$14.99
00333922	Frozen 2	$14.99
00702286	Glee	$16.99
00702160	The Great American Country Songbook	$19.99
00702148	Great American Gospel for Guitar	$14.99
00702050	Great Classical Themes for Easy Guitar	$9.99
00148030	Halloween Guitar Songs	$17.99
00702273	Irish Songs	$14.99
00192503	Jazz Classics for Easy Guitar	$16.99
00702275	Jazz Favorites for Easy Guitar	$17.99
00702274	Jazz Standards for Easy Guitar	$19.99
00702162	Jumbo Easy Guitar Songbook	$24.99
00232285	La La Land	$16.99
00702258	Legends of Rock	$14.99
00702189	MTV's 100 Greatest Pop Songs	$34.99
00702272	1950s Rock	$16.99
00702271	1960s Rock	$16.99
00702270	1970s Rock	$24.99
00702269	1980s Rock	$16.99

00702268	1990s Rock	$24.99
00369043	Rock Songs for Kids	$14.99
00109725	Once	$14.99
00702187	Selections from O Brother Where Art Thou?	$19.99
00702178	100 Songs for Kids	$16.99
00702515	Pirates of the Caribbean	$17.99
00702125	Praise and Worship for Guitar	$14.99
00287930	Songs from *A Star Is Born, The Greatest Showman, La La Land,* and More Movie Musicals	$16.99
00702285	Southern Rock Hits	$12.99
00156420	Star Wars Music	$16.99
00121535	30 Easy Celtic Guitar Solos	$16.99
00244654	Top Hits of 2017	$14.99
00283786	Top Hits of 2018	$14.99
00302269	Top Hits of 2019	$14.99
00355779	Top Hits of 2020	$14.99
00374083	Top Hits of 2021	$16.99
00702294	Top Worship Hits	$17.99
00702255	VH1's 100 Greatest Hard Rock Songs	$39.99
00702175	VH1's 100 Greatest Songs of Rock and Roll	$34.99
00702253	Wicked	$12.99

ARTIST COLLECTIONS

00702267	AC/DC for Easy Guitar	$17.99
00156221	Adele – 25	$16.99
00396889	Adele – 30	$19.99
00702040	Best of the Allman Brothers	$16.99
00702865	J.S. Bach for Easy Guitar	$15.99
00702169	Best of The Beach Boys	$16.99
00702292	The Beatles — 1	$22.99
00125796	Best of Chuck Berry	$16.99
00702201	The Essential Black Sabbath	$15.99
00702250	blink-182 — Greatest Hits	$19.99
02501615	Zac Brown Band — The Foundation	$19.99
02501621	Zac Brown Band — You Get What You Give	$16.99
00702043	Best of Johnny Cash	$19.99
00702090	Eric Clapton's Best	$16.99
00702086	Eric Clapton — from the Album Unplugged	$17.99
00702202	The Essential Eric Clapton	$19.99
00702053	Best of Patsy Cline	$17.99
00222697	Very Best of Coldplay – 2nd Edition	$17.99
00702229	The Very Best of Creedence Clearwater Revival	$16.99
00702145	Best of Jim Croce	$16.99
00702278	Crosby, Stills & Nash	$12.99
14042809	Bob Dylan	$15.99
00702276	Fleetwood Mac — Easy Guitar Collection	$17.99
00139462	The Very Best of Grateful Dead	$17.99
00702136	Best of Merle Haggard	$19.99
00702227	Jimi Hendrix — Smash Hits	$19.99
00702288	Best of Hillsong United	$12.99
00702236	Best of Antonio Carlos Jobim	$15.99

00702245	Elton John — Greatest Hits 1970–2002	$19.99
00129855	Jack Johnson	$17.99
00702204	Robert Johnson	$16.99
00702234	Selections from Toby Keith — 35 Biggest Hits	$12.95
00702003	Kiss	$16.99
00702216	Lynyrd Skynyrd	$17.99
00702182	The Essential Bob Marley	$17.99
00146081	Maroon 5	$14.99
00121925	Bruno Mars — Unorthodox Jukebox	$12.99
00702248	Paul McCartney — All the Best	$14.99
00125484	The Best of MercyMe	$12.99
00702209	Steve Miller Band — Young Hearts (Greatest Hits)	$12.95
00124167	Jason Mraz	$15.99
00702096	Best of Nirvana	$17.99
00702211	The Offspring — Greatest Hits	$17.99
00138026	One Direction	$17.99
00702030	Best of Roy Orbison	$17.99
00702144	Best of Ozzy Osbourne	$14.99
00702279	Tom Petty	$17.99
00102911	Pink Floyd	$17.99
00702139	Elvis Country Favorites	$19.99
00702293	The Very Best of Prince	$22.99
00699415	Best of Queen for Guitar	$16.99
00109279	Best of R.E.M.	$14.99
00702208	Red Hot Chili Peppers — Greatest Hits	$19.99
00198960	The Rolling Stones	$17.99
00174793	The Very Best of Santana	$16.99
00702196	Best of Bob Seger	$16.99
00146046	Ed Sheeran	$19.99

00702252	Frank Sinatra — Nothing But the Best	$12.99
00702010	Best of Rod Stewart	$17.99
00702049	Best of George Strait	$17.99
00702259	Taylor Swift for Easy Guitar	$15.99
00359800	Taylor Swift – Easy Guitar Anthology	$24.99
00702260	Taylor Swift — Fearless	$14.99
00139727	Taylor Swift — 1989	$19.99
00115960	Taylor Swift — Red	$16.99
00253667	Taylor Swift — Reputation	$17.99
00702290	Taylor Swift — Speak Now	$16.99
00232849	Chris Tomlin Collection – 2nd Edition	$14.99
00702226	Chris Tomlin — See the Morning	$12.95
00148643	Train	$14.99
00702427	U2 — 18 Singles	$19.99
00702108	Best of Stevie Ray Vaughan	$17.99
00279005	The Who	$14.99
00702123	Best of Hank Williams	$15.99
00194548	Best of John Williams	$14.99
00702228	Neil Young — Greatest Hits	$17.99
00119133	Neil Young — Harvest	$16.99

Prices, contents and availability subject to change without notice.

HAL•LEONARD®

Visit Hal Leonard online at halleonard.com

REALLY EASY GUITAR

Easy-to-follow charts to get you playing right away are presented in these collections of arrangements in chords, lyrics and basic tab for all guitarists.

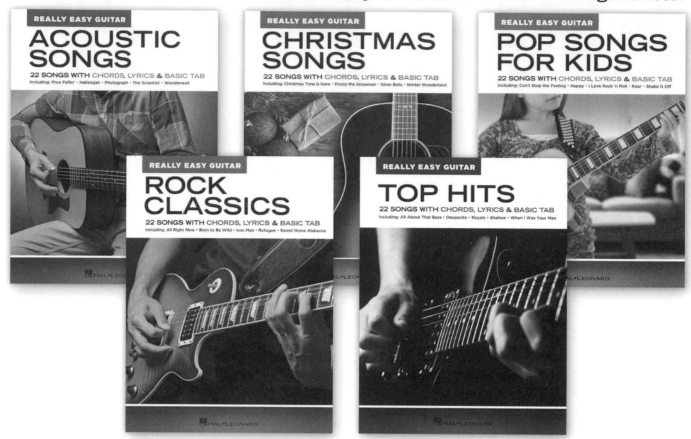

ACOUSTIC CLASSICS
22 songs: Angie • Best of My Love • Dust in the Wind • Fire and Rain • A Horse with No Name • Layla • More Than a Feeling • Night Moves • Patience • Time in a Bottle • Wanted Dead or Alive • and more.
00300600 .... $9.99

ACOUSTIC SONGS
22 songs: Free Fallin' • Good Riddance (Time of Your Life) • Hallelujah • I'm Yours • Losing My Religion • Mr. Jones • Photograph • Riptide • The Scientist • Wonderwall • and more.
00286663 .... $10.99

ADELE
22 songs: All I Ask • Chasing Pavements • Daydreamer • Easy On Me • Hello • I Drink Wine • Love in the Dark • Lovesong • Make You Feel My Love • Turning Tables • Water Under the Bridge • and more.
00399557 .... $12.99

THE BEATLES FOR KIDS
14 songs: All You Need Is Love • Blackbird • Good Day Sunshine • Here Comes the Sun • I Want to Hold Your Hand • Let It Be • With a Little Help from My Friends • Yellow Submarine • and more.
00346031 .... $12.99

CHRISTMAS CLASSICS
22 Christmas carols: Away in a Manger • Deck the Hall • It Came upon the Midnight Clear • Jingle Bells • Silent Night • The Twelve Days of Christmas • We Wish You a Merry Christmas • and more.
00348327 .... $10.99

CHRISTMAS SONGS
22 holiday favorites: Blue Christmas • Christmas Time Is Here • Frosty the Snowman • Have Yourself a Merry Little Christmas • Mary, Did You Know? • Silver Bells • Winter Wonderland • and more.
00294775 .... $9.99

THE DOORS
22 songs: Break on Through to the Other Side • Hello, I Love You (Won't You Tell Me Your Name?) • L.A. Woman • Light My Fire • Love Her Madly • People Are Strange • Riders on the Storm • Touch Me • and more.
00345890 .... $9.99

BILLIE EILISH
14 songs: All the Good Girls Go to Hell • Bad Guy • Everything I Wanted • Idontwannabeyouanymore • No Time to Die • Ocean Eyes • Six Feet Under • Wish You Were Gay • and more.
00346351 .... $12.99

POP SONGS FOR KIDS
22 songs: Brave • Can't Stop the Feeling • Happy • I Love Rock 'N Roll • Let It Go • Roar • Shake It Off • We Got the Beat • and more.
00286698 .... $10.99

ROCK CLASSICS
22 songs: All Right Now • Born to Be Wild • Don't Fear the Reaper • Hey Joe • Iron Man • Old Time Rock & Roll • Refugee • Sweet Home Alabama • You Shook Me All Night Long • and more.
00286699 .... $10.99

TAYLOR SWIFT
22 hits: Back to December • Cardigan • Exile • Look What You Made Me Do • Mean • The One • Our Song • Safe & Sound • Teardrops on My Guitar • We Are Never Ever Getting Back Together • White Horse • You Need to Calm Down • and more.
00356881 .... $12.99

TOP HITS
22 hits: All About That Bass • All of Me • Despacito • Love Yourself • Royals • Say Something • Shallow • Someone like You • This Is Me • A Thousand Years • When I Was Your Man • and more.
00300599 .... $10.99

HAL•LEONARD®
halleonard.com

Prices, contents and availability subject to change without notice. All prices listed in U.S. funds.